To Chers
my little sweetie
& good friend along
the path

John Shiff

7/2005

Beyond Religion

Talks between Two Priests:
One Episcopal, the Other
Zen-Buddhist.

By Ashley C. Neal and John C. Seniff

Copyright © 2004 by
Ashley C. Neal & John C. Seniff

ISBN 0-7414-2014-7

Photographs © by John C. Seniff

Published by:

INFINITY
PUBLISHING.COM

1094 New Dehaven Street
Suite 100
West Conshohocken, PA 19428-2713
Info@buybooksontheweb.com
www.buybooksontheweb.com
Toll-free (877) BUY BOOK
Local Phone (610) 941-9999
Fax (610) 941-9959

Printed in the United States of America

Printed on Recycled Paper

Published May 2004

To Bob, Christine, Clare, Connie,
Don, Gordon, Jack, Lindsay,
Maya & Rico,

Only he who, while fully recognizing and understanding his Western heritage, penetrates and absorbs the heritage of the East, can gain the highest values of both worlds and do justice to them. East and West are the two halves of our human consciousness, comparable to the two poles of a magnet, which condition and correspond to each other and cannot be separated. Only if man realizes this fact will he become a complete human being.

-Lama Anagarika Govinda,
Creative Meditation and Multi-Dimensional Consciousness

Beyond Religion

Contents

Introduction:

Setting the Stage

I am an Episcopal priest and my co-author, John Seniff, is a Zen Buddhist priest. We were introduced through a mutual friend in the Episcopal Church, yet curiously our meeting was predicted by a former parishioner of mine five years earlier. She came to report she'd seen it, along with some other things including the genesis of this book, in a vision. I'm reminded of the line in that Paul Simon song, "These are the days of miracles and wonders...." I'd quite forgotten the whole incident until after I met John. Then, when I mentioned it to him, his response was, "Well, you conjured me up somehow!" The mind is very interesting.

John was ordained a Zen Buddhist priest in the Mahayana tradition after over a quarter century of study. Having lived in India in his youth, he has also been strongly influenced by Hindu philosophy and the work of J. Krishnamurti, Nisargadatta Maharaj and Ramana Maharshi. He is also a confirmed Episcopalian who studied for a time as a Benedictine monk; thus his background in Christianity also contributes much to these talks.

In my early years of ordained ministry I was involved in ecumenical and inter-religious dialogue. When I learned that John was also interested in dialogue, I invited him to work on this book. John was immediately open to the project. My agenda was to compare notes, to widen the scope of our understanding, to share common ground and to broaden my own scope by learning from another spiritual tradition. I did not know that I would be engaged in a different sort of dialogue from the kind I had been used to.

My experience in dialogue was of the traditional institutional ecclesiastical variety. That is, we would get together and talk with the purpose of comparing notes and hopefully coming to some consensus. John's experience, on the other hand, came from his years of participation with dialogue groups in the Krishnamurti tradition. I knew a little about the Indian teacher

Krishnamurti's work, but only from a cursory look at his books some years earlier. I had no actual experience with this sort of dialogue.

Though they changed over time, our early talks had the character of the Krishnamurti dialogue. I came to realize that I would have to change...to let go of my preconceptions, ideas and so on. This was going to be much more difficult than I had imagined. It felt like being back in seminary only this time instead of being programmed, I was being de-programmed.

> ...everybody has different assumptions and opinions...it is important to see that the different opinions you have are the result of your past thought: all your experiences... That is all programmed into your memory.... Opinions thus tend to be experienced as 'truths'....you got them from your teacher, your family, or by reading... Then for one reason or another you are identified with them and you defend them.... If we defend our opinions in this way, we are not going to be able to have a dialogue. And we are often unconsciously defending our opinions....[i]

Yet, as it evolved, our work went beyond dialogue. Instead of talks between two equals, as I had thought they would be at first, they became talks between student and teacher. I was learning new ways of seeing and being.

John once shared something that his teacher had said to him. "Be surprised by nothing." I try to practice that now.

The impact of this work is both individual and collective. We should know that without a fundamental change in the hearts and minds of individuals, change cannot and will not be achieved in our world. Our conflicting religious worldviews are at the center of the problem of the world and thus must be at the center of the solution. I have long felt that our competing internal and external views of reality, not Reality itself, are a direct cause of the suffering of this world. If we could understand this basic point, then we might be able to have a more peaceful, sane and realistic life.

These talks have helped me to explore this fundamental question of Reality from various viewpoints. They have encouraged and challenged me to examine my own concepts, ideas and opinions and in doing so I have begun to resolve some of those conflicts and to have begun to make that connection to Self that John talks about.

The church can no longer claim sovereign status in this global environment. It is an institution in which out worn structures are crumbling. But new wineskins will give forth new wine. We should be surprised by nothing. And while we need relinquish neither tradition nor foundation as we move into the uncharted territory ahead, we must be diligent in our effort to interpret the Christian story for a new generation in a new world setting.

My desire was to participate in a dialogue that was effective. I have done this and more. As stated repeatedly in this book, it begins with the individual. God, the Self, is found within. Hearts are changed within. This is not a book about changing the world, nor so much about changing institutions, but about being changed ourselves.

The title of this book "Beyond Religion" grew out of one of our talks. One day, John said to me, "It's not about religion, Ashley. It's beyond religion." That's when I knew what we would call this book. For much of what we discuss is, in this way, "beyond religion." It is my hope that insights and questions will be raised in the minds and hearts of readers who have struggled with their own search for God or for enlightenment, especially coming out of a Western Christian background.

I invite the reader to join me on this adventure of the Spirit, and I wish you encouragement on your path.

- Ashley C. Neal
Amelia Island, Florida

Part One:

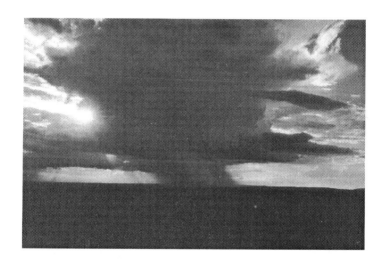

Transitions

It was the week before Easter, 2001, when I drove out to New Mexico from Florida to meet John in Santa Fe. He was going to show me how to get to the Monastery of Christ in the Desert in Abiquiu. It's a bit of a drive down to the bottom of a canyon in the middle of Georgia O'Keefe country. This was a place he had visited many times over the years and where I was going to spend Easter Week on retreat, while John went camping in the desert. I had taken a sabbatical that year from parish ministry. After a decade of hard work, this road trip felt like an adventure worthy of pursuit. As it turned out it was. I saw some of the most heavenly landscapes imaginable during my time in New Mexico and met some interesting people along the way.

There were no other guests when I arrived.... I was assigned to the guest suite overlooking the canyon. Later another guest came. She had driven 900 miles non-stop from Los Angeles, she said, after having had a vision that she was supposed to go to the desert to meet a "poet and a visionary." She said she didn't know where she was driving as she'd never been to this part of the country before, but that her car had just taken her there to the monastery. We talked for a while and then she left saying she'd be heading back to California the next morning as she'd seen what she had come there to see. She said she was very glad to have met us. It was a curious encounter, but we all had the sense that it was meant to be.

The next day, sitting on the porch behind the guest suite at the monastery, in the desert overlooking the canyon, enjoying the tortillas and beer bought in the town of Chimayo, which we had visited along the way...John and I enjoyed both the food and the conversation.

Desert Talk

J: Don't you think Ashley, that Jesus would have eaten a bologna sandwich?

A: I definitely think so.

J: When you're here in the desert and you're hungry...so many things taste good. Things you normally wouldn't think about. You just suddenly like it because you have it with you. Having a bologna with...we should give the recipe.

A: Definitely. Please, give the recipe.

J: The "Desert Sandwich," is bologna on top of a banana tortilla. It's very important to get banana tortillas.

A: From the tortilla factory.

J: From Leona's tortilla factory in Chimayo, New Mexico. She might have to go back to the freezer to get them for you. So, you have the bologna on top of the banana tortilla. Then you grab those little packets of mayonnaise and mustard. Make sure you keep them in your car just in case. You spread them in the middle of the bologna making a little streak. Then you turn half the bologna on top of the other half, and you squish it back and forth, so it spreads...(laughing). It's a very important technique, to do it just right.

A: No cutlery, by the way.

J: No cutlery, nothing at this point. Then you take cheddar cheese or the cheese of your choice.

A: Sharp.

J: Yes, sharp is good. Pick it up at the convenience store and bring a pocketknife. You have a choice of putting it in the middle and rolling it into the bologna, the mustard and the mayonnaise or else having the cheese on the side. It's like a sushi roll. Don't forget to have it with a beer. Beer is very, very good with this sandwich.

A: We should probably also say that this monastery uses instant coffee, and that we had to rely on a special way of making a decent cup of coffee.

J: For those that know coffee, instant gets old really fast. There is an alternative to a hot pot that has an adapter that you stick into the lighter of your car. It's perfect. But make sure to start the engine, because I've had the experience before of having the battery drained and being stuck in the middle of nowhere and not being able to start the car. I had a good cup of coffee but....

A: ...but, you were stuck in the desert with a drained battery!

J: I was. So, do it while your engine is running. It takes about ten minutes. Heat up the water and then take your own fine ground coffee with one of those cup-sized plastic cone holders. Once the water is hot you pull it out. Keep your engine running for a little while to charge it up again. Pour in the coffee, cream, sugar or however you like it. Find a cup with a good lid, from either Starbuck's or another gourmet coffee place. Keep it so that you can pour your coffee into it. That keeps it warmer. Or, use a thermos if you have one. Then have yourself a fresh cup of coffee.

A: A perfect way to start the day! Now, John, yesterday we stopped off and visited a place near here where you lived for a while.

J: In Abiquiu?

A: Right. We visited the lady who lives in the house you used to live in. She told me that you are famous in these parts for something you did here ten years ago. She said you brought a ham in here and that the brothers were still talking about it this year, just two days ago at Easter. I'm curious. Why would this monastery remember you because of a ten-year-old ham?

J: It was a new innovation to a routine that they have of eating soy mush. Actually, they have soy roll, fake meat loaf with ketchup on top. This woman had a deli in Albuquerque, and we thought it would be nice to bring a ham into the monastery.

A: But isn't that contraband in this vegetarian monastery?

J: Apparently they used to have meat on special days. I don't know if they still do. Usually it was chicken. But to bring in a whole pork ham was very, very good. I think everybody was on a pork high after eating it. When we went to her house yesterday, she told us that they were still talking about that. It's kind of like us talking about the bologna sandwich, and how good it was. Take it out of its context and it's new, it's fresh.

A: It's difficult for people to find new and fresh things in a culture where you can find anything, anytime.

J: You can go to a store and have some good fresh produce or meat, but it's your mind that goes to the rotten section unfortunately, and doesn't keep that newness and freshness, that element of surprise. When it happens, it happens. It's not something you plan. We don't think, "These bologna sandwiches or this ham are going to be good." No, it just happens. It's there, it's simple and it's easy to make. You take a bite and it brings you to another level.

A: Like a spiritual experience.

J: Pretty close.

A: Jesus would have liked a bologna and cheese sandwich!

J: I think Jesus would be sitting here, probably drinking a beer, eating a bologna sandwich and getting a little bit tired of routines. It's hard for me to see Jesus in a routine. There were a lot of surprises in his life. For somebody to box that, to package that into some sort of form, seems to go against what he was showing in his actions: Packaging Jesus, packaging spirituality, packaging learning.

A: I spent an hour and a half this morning in the chapel. That can become a trap if we're not careful. It seems that human beings want to tame things, to make things routine, to give things form and structure.

J: I'm sitting here looking at these ants out here. They have a routine, specified way of doing things. We aren't ants, but we've made life into routine. There's a great movie about chaos, or "life in turmoil" that was made about ten or fifteen years ago. What the filmmaker did in this film was to show everyday life in different parts of the world. One of the things you saw in cities around the world was people running around like ants. They'd wake up at a certain time. They'd go this way and that way. To do that day in and day out, there has got to be some sort of insanity there. It goes against human nature.

A: People are getting sick.

J: Obviously that's a sign. People are getting sick, having heart attacks, high blood pressure or not eating well and trying to find some other kind of life, where they are eating right, getting exercise and all that.

A: But here you say Jesus brings in the new. That is so connected to health, to the deepest level of who we are as human beings. It seems that we can't do it ourselves, though. Or can we?

J: It seems that we're left to trying to do it ourselves. In this society, there is no one supporting your way of being different. Those are the very people that are immersed in the social world. The system doesn't support that. To have some sort of support, some kind of encouragement to find something different in your way, in your own unique way.

A: Religious systems talk about unconditional love, yet unconditional love is love that frees a person to become.

J: From where does that unconditional love arise?

A: It comes from the Source of being.

J: If that Source of being is there, it must have to do with one's Self, only one's Self. Not the being of somebody else, but the Source that springs out of you.

A: It is not easy to locate that Source.

J: It's not an easy thing as long as you remain within that same pattern. You begin to see it as you go out of the pattern. When you are standing more and more on your own feet, then there's another dimension. Entering into that other dimension becomes difficult, but then you recognize your own unique way of dealing with whatever it is that you're trying to find. It certainly comes with some sort of conflict, like hitting a wall. You come through one door, and then you hit another wall. You come past that and then something else comes up. That is all springing from your self, from your own mind, thoughts and emotions. It becomes the interior world that you struggle with. Those are the thoughts, the emotions, the feelings and the mind stuff. You are left with just yourself.

You have a struggle going on. As a human being, you feel you are part of this world, part of society. In a sense, this world becomes your universe. But then you begin to see that this world is very limited. It presses down on you. This world, in which you were, begins to crumble. It's like the party is over.

A: So, this world is oppressing you?

J: Take a normal person doing normal things; elementary school, high school, birthday parties, going to college, getting that first job, that first car or house, getting married, and so on. As time goes on they begin to see that it's limited, and they begin to wonder about its meaning. Something may begin to fester in them. They may think, "This doesn't seem to be the endless universe anymore, it's very limited." Then he or she begins to pursue a different way, a different path. They want to find this other universe. This was their world before. Now they have to look for this other world, but they don't know this other world that they are searching for. The danger is that when you begin to walk in that direction, somebody or some organization comes along or something snatches you up, and you begin to lose that initiative. You become dependent.

A: It is quite easy to turn away from the internal process when it's difficult or painful. People are naturally averse to pain. They don't just get snatched up unwillingly, do they? That person is making a decision that this is as far as they want to go on this new path.

J: Some people do snatch you up I think. Some organizations or teachers try to snatch you up. You may fall into situations while feeling vulnerable. You think, "What do I do now?" Then something comes along and you say, "Let me try this." You give it a shot, and the next thing you know you're trapped by that very thing.

It seems to happen a lot with spiritual groups. You go along, and you're questioning at first. But then you find you're really in it and it's a really hard place to get out of. There may be something that you totally disagree with or something that causes you some real pain and so you leave feeling distraught, maybe violated too. The important thing is to know that you allowed yourself to get into that. You pursued it. Unfortunately it took a sledgehammer to hit you over the head, to hurt you and to get you out of it. Hopefully then, that person will pick up and begin to use that as a big lesson. It's a very tricky, slippery thing and one can easily fall back.

A: People still go out and create structures and then develop these dependencies. It seems nothing will change that.

J: Yes. Then it becomes your routine way of living. You become used to it and take it for granted.

A: What would be the way to avoid that?

J: Pinch yourself in the butt ten times a day! Keep the Bodhisattva vow of keeping study high, but help low: The study of your Self, of your life, that you must keep very, very high. Keep low another person or others helping you. Most important is the study of one's Self. "To study the Way is to study the Self," as Zen teacher Dogen said. It's very, very important that you keep that high. Never forget that.

> *Back in Florida, John and I met most mornings,*
> *always over a cup of coffee. The natural scenery*
> *was beautiful; a porch overlooking a lagoon with*
> *wonderful water birds and constantly changing*
> *weather. There was always something to look at*
> *and observe. Our conversations emerged In the*
> *midst of this picture-postcard scenery.*

Go forth and Organize?

A: The way of Jesus wasn't a religion in the sense of an organization.

J: Religion gets organized, institutionalized and put into a system. Then only the system, the outer shell is maintained.

A: The outer shell has no necessary bearing on the essential content of the religion. What do we do? Erase all institutions, and human beings keep creating them.

J: Take the institution of the family. I learned to be careful as a psychotherapist working with families. You can get sucked in. Like the family, organized religion is a world unto itself, in which certain ways of being, doing and thinking are all linked up. It is important to honestly see what is going on.

A: Congregations are like families. Being and doing become norms and rules, then those become the way. Each congregation creates an identity for itself according to its own particular worldview, its own brand of the religion. It's a problem. As soon as you get people together...

J: ...yes, they...

A: ... start distorting.

J: What my Zen teacher would call homogeneous thinking.

A: Group-think?

J: Yes, where they say, "Okay, we're going to do this, " or "That Mr. X is bad, we're going to kill him." And everybody says, "Yeah, let's kill him!" What happened differently, I think, when Christ came, was the element of reflection. Instead of everyone tribally saying, "Let's kill that person," one person said, "Well I don't know, maybe we should think about that." Christ said, "Love your enemy." Reflection came into play. "Love my enemy? How can I?" I believe this was a huge evolutionary transition. The tables were turned. With this reflective ability came compassion and wisdom. All it took was one individual to create a domino effect.

A: That reflection allows for independent versus homogeneous thinking. Jesus challenged people to think, reflect and critique for themselves.

J: Christ encouraged his disciples to believe in themselves, to think and to question. It is commonly thought that Christ meant for people to follow him in his way, as if he was the only way. That is not what he was saying. Putting this person in authority gives power to these groups to control others. Organized religions are the pedestal. They sustain people's projections instead of helping them get to the true and the Real.

A: How do you interpret the saying, "I am the Way, the Truth and the Light?" and "The only way to the Father is through me?" from John's gospel (14:6.)

J: To mean "I am you, and you are me. We are inside each other, and through each other. "Me" is not a separate entity. Thomas says, "How can we know where you are going? We do not know the way?" Jesus confronts the question head on. "If you get who I am, you get who you are." The only way you can do that is to get past your projections, concepts, beliefs, feelings and personal views. They put him on a pedestal by seeing things in their own way instead of seeing what he was trying to show them about himself, or seeing him as he really was.

Isn't the best educational situation one in which the children are allowed to learn, discover and experience for themselves? That is the only way to learn, because it encourages that reflective ability and questioning. In questioning differences, we begin to see the sameness and the inter-relationship of things. We discover that interconnectedness, and through you, the world evolves.

Freedom

A: Let's talk about freedom and what that is.

J: When I hear about spiritual freedom, it sounds like enlightenment.

Freedom, we could say, is freedom from being enslaved outwardly and freedom from being enslaved inwardly. In our culture we have a sense that there is more freedom. We are not enslaved by a tyrannical government or dictatorship. We can travel from state to state, and do things that we would never be able to do in other countries. Here in the United States and parts of Europe, in Asia too, there is a certain amount of freedom. At the same time, there are restrictions, regulations and rules.

But freedom has a ring in people's ears: Freedom to go from this place to that place, or do this thing or that thing. This is a very big ideal for Americans.

Yet, somehow there is still a sense of un-freedom. There is a sense of being caught. There is the internal state, and the person who wants to do something about it. There is difficulty or confusion, because it doesn't seem to work in the same way, as fighting a government or organization to get freedom, to achieve the political or environmental freedom to do what one wants or needs to do. It is a different kind of thing. It's a solitary thing, based completely on your self, not dependent on somebody else, or working as a group or drawing from other sources to fight an unjust cause.

It's something that comes up in your system, in your way. So, we find a limitation in the freedom that is given us. Especially when thinking about our mortality. We know that we have only a certain time to live and we want somehow, someway to get the most meaning from our lives. We may not be clear about it but there is something in a person that has an internal awareness and knowledge of that.

Some people may go along in their lives and say to themselves, "I have what I need, but I don't feel particularly free," or "What is the meaning of my life?"

In finding internal freedom, if something rings true for you, then you hear it, not just hearing physically with your ears, or seeing physically with your eyes. Say you're reading something in Christianity, Buddhism, or Zen and something rings true for you and you get meaning from that. You feel connected to that. If that is strong enough in you, you will want to pursue it. It depends on the individual, how far they are willing to take it and how much they want to know.

A: We have the idea in Christianity of grace, of a movement beyond the individual self. It seems that the strength and degree of one's internal response is beyond the individual's will or capacity in and of themselves.

J: Do you mean to say that it requires something more?

A: Yes, our abilities to receive differ. We have different capacities to understand, to hear or to even have this movement beyond the individual self.

J: Yes.

A: We could say, "It's not my movement happening, but God's movement in me, allowing me to see, to understand, to hear and to respond."

J: That is an important point. Each individual is unique. We all have certain capacities, to use that word. What is important along this journey is that you will realize your capacity. Unfortunately, what I see in some of these groups and spiritual leaders is that they believe that they have a greater capacity than they really have. Say they have a very high IQ, and they're very good academically, or they have a skill for public speaking. Then they feel that they can go out with this particular skill, with this little part that they understand, and begin to teach other people.

A: So the teacher is caught already.

J: Well, they're not even teachers. They're saying they're teachers and they've got other people saying it.

14

Being in the present, in the true sense of the word, is not just watching whether your cup is going to spill the coffee. The present moment is the present of knowing. Because you can see a lot in your self, that extends and brings in the past and future.

Let's say, in therapy that you want to go into the past, and study your childhood. There is some value in that. But if you are able to see everything clearly now, everything, all one thing in this one time, then you can see your self very much as a whole, rather than as the fragmented aspects that we usually see as ourselves.

A: So, freedom, in this way, is found in the Now?

J: That's true on one level. Unfortunately it's become a banner that's waved. "Be present, that's your true being." But there's more to it than that. That's why I say there's more to it for example than bringing the coffee cup, or "Now we're going to do walking meditation," or "See yourself as you dip your hand into the water." That's just mind stuff. That's mind fragmenting itself, thinking "Present." "Be in the present. Be in the NOW!" But, we have to understand that it is much, much more than that. I can't believe that the Universal Truth is so simply understood. Just with our minds. Just with our brains. That we stop there. There's something funny about that. Then people rush to make some kind of modality, spiritual practice or lifestyle. There's an element of it that sounds true, but it doesn't complete the whole picture.

A: It sounds hopeless from a human point of view. There is no spiritual discipline that I can practice to understand this.

J: It's like my teacher would say, "Trust in your ignorance." It's not going to help you eat your food any better or breathe air any better, or take your bath any better. You already have everything in that sense. In the most profound deep sense, you have everything already. Trust your ignorance. It's better to not know, rather than to know something in the wrong way and then go and intoxicate other people with half-baked or burnt to the crisp knowledge. Be careful of intoxicants.

Faith

A warlord invaded a village and killed most of the inhabitants. The remaining villagers fled, except for the Zen master who continued to sit in the temple. The warlord stormed up to the temple brandishing his sword and cried, "Don't you know that you are looking at someone who could run you through with my sword without batting an eye?" The Zen master replied, "Don't you know that you are looking at someone who could be run through without batting an eye?" Thereupon the warlord bowed and withdrew.

-Source unknown

A: In places where people no longer feel obliged to go to church for social reasons, I imagine they are there seeking faith.

J: This question of faith is tricky. What exactly is faith in the Christian context?

A: One of the meanings is trust.

J: So the priest would tell the congregation to trust God, and that is what's good for you. Is that faith?

A: It might be. Some pastors might say that, though faith is generally considered a gift. It's not something we can get or have on our own.

J: Faith is taking a risk. Here questioning the church might be equivalent to being untrusting or unfaithful.

A: Some people have, I think, disowned their internal voice, their internal knowledge and sense of God within. They have been discouraged from practicing faith in a mature way.

J: Faith in that way is like a child showing trust in the parents?

A: Yes. In this case the clergy, and "god," become perpetual parents and people become perpetual children.

J: To be rebellious would be rocking the boat.

A: You risk being labeled a non-conformist, or a heretic. As we know, institutions have gone to great lengths to silence individual voices to perpetuate a collective illusion of rightness. Yet faith is ultimately faith in one's self and in the pursuit of God. Individual conscience is always the highest guide in the end.

J: If I listen to you, you say something that rings true to me, I take hold of that and use that in my own way. I have faith in myself and I don't have to be dependent on you to tell me more.

A: But faith is more than psychological maturity. It is inclusive of the Universal.

J: So, there is something larger than your perceived self?

A: Yes.

J: Call it Universal Truth or something.

A: To me that should be the work of the church, to help people to connect with the Self, with the Divine.

J: Well, I agree. If you do actually have faith...as a particular person, you have to trust yourself. I listen to this Universal Truth. Somebody has to take the actions. It is that person.

A: The risk of going inward to make this connection to the Self is also the risk of going outward.

J: It's simultaneous. We think of outward actions, one's willingness to risk by giving away one's money, for example. Yet, the risk is first inward. Outward actions are the expression of the inward willingness to risk. The real risk is going through the un-layering of one's perceived self, because one is committed to making contact with something greater. In this, one is risking everything. Faith then has this element of risk.

To do that is to take that step forward. The more steps we take, the more un-layering, meaning un-layering of your preconceived viewpoints, your opinions, all those things that you felt made up you, and that you felt were so important. Now you're willing to risk un-layering those, and going forward. And not knowing.... That is the important thing.

A: Yes, or it's not faith.

J: There can be a certain amount of risk taken when other things are fine in your life and you feel like you can put this thing at risk because you have these structures and places to depend on. There are different levels of risking. Then there is the risking of all, which is the big Risk. You have no foundation to stand on anymore. Your foundations begin to crumble and to dismantle themselves. That is when other dimensions begin to enter in, that you hadn't seen before. You have passed this one or two-dimensional world, and now you're getting into some third or fourth dimension of reality. Other things begin to come in and show themselves, maybe not such pleasant things. It is hard, in this sense.

A: You're only fooling yourself if you think its going to be anything but a relinquishing of your attachments. Your idea of what you thought was reality goes. This is why Jesus talks about counting the cost. If you are seeking faith, you need to know that it is going to cost you. Count the cost before you embark on the trip.

J: I've heard it in other ways from sages or teachers who say, "Do you really want this?" Maybe what you really want is over there. Maybe you want a better kind of life, and to just ease some of the things that have been burdening you.

In my relationship with my teacher, there was the practice, the *zazen*, the sitting meditation and the chanting. Then there was work, mostly gardening and cutting wood. Then there were also long hours of Ping-Pong. It was every day living along with some study. Later I studied the classics in more detail, but in the beginning it was an everyday matter. I would come in and say; "Well what do you see for me in such and such situation?" Things were dealt with in everyday language. Very little was said about the other Zen Masters, or the patriarchs, or what the Scriptures or Sutras said.

One of the key points was learning to be critical. I don't mean cynical criticism, but critical about looking at one's self and at the world. It was important to delve into understanding that.

You're really looking at things with an eye of strength, an eye of clarity. Underneath, what I learned from my teacher was from his character, from who he was. He rarely wore robes, only if he was to go out and speak and even then he usually wore regular clothes and smoked his Carlton cigarettes. There wasn't anything showy or pretentious about him at all.

I have to thank God, to thank Buddha, that there wasn't that element. That I didn't walk into some other Zen community, with those pseudo-trappings. Here was a man who was just living his life, along with the other person who was studying with him. It was certainly very difficult being with him, but it felt genuine...real. At the same time, the message given either directly or indirectly was, "John, you are your own hero. You are that yourself. Get this message." That was expressed firmly over and over and over again.

Once, from New Mexico, I talked to him and he said, "John, what separates you from these other so-called Zen people, is the willingness to really risk your life for what you believe." He wasn't saying necessarily that I should risk my physical life, but rather that it is about being obedient and being willing to risk what it is in me....

A: Everything.

J: Yes. And it doesn't mean some big heroic gesture. It may involve something like that, I don't know, like to die on the cross. The risking of your comfort, your routine, and the life you are used to living. It's the risking of your world.

A: I don't think Jesus started out thinking that he would die on the cross. He was just going along, creating effects. Circumstances came up, people felt threatened and there was the rising up of fear. Fear is always at the heart of resistance to change and transformation.

J: Yes and the fear is the unwillingness to risk.

A: If you really understand that, then it means something practical. I think what he is saying about risking your life, is being willing to take those steps. Instead of getting to a point and saying, "I'm not willing to go to that next step," because of the fear.

J: Fear seems like a tangible thing. For example we have people who go to the church, and this is part of their whole function in life. If they were actually to let this go and change, there would be fear. Yes, there would be fear. But before that, there is something that is stopping...

A: ...before the fear?

J: Before the fear, there is something. It is like this wave of what we call normalcy. There is an old Chinese or Sanskrit saying that the devil takes on the appearance of the normalcy of life, which in turn steals your life.

Let's say for example, there are basic functions in life, food, shelter and clothing. In order to have these things, we work together in farming, in building houses and having things. We keep contractual agreements about certain things. You're not going to steal the crops early. The world in its outward normalcy and our concerns, are an external way of living and being with things. What happens in the normalcy is that we get stuck in the outward process of life. We think that the answers to our questions and problems are going to be solved outwardly.

The other way is not externally driven. It's the risk of going inward. That puts you in a different framework. You don't have a chart or a diagram, although some people will try to make diagrams in the process and then get trapped in the diagrams, and more diagrams.

A: When you go within, the change in your relationship with the external changes your entire perception of reality and your way of relating to the world.

J: That's right. As long as your world is just an outward world, and the world is limited by outside functioning. We begin by going within, in another direction, and there is a change in the perception of the outward world. The outward world begins then to become a teacher, because it reflects back to you something about your self. That is when the world, the phenomenon, becomes substance, and then gives meaning. One is all and all is one.

This aspect of seeing and relating to the phenomena in a different way than you ever have before, is something that I would say, though I have seen certain elements of it in other religions or spiritual practices, is very unique to Zen.

We human beings relate to the phenomena. We experience the world through our senses. Here emotions, feelings and thoughts come into play. What is different though is that your relationship to phenomena is like your relationship to your parents in the sense that you came from your parents at birth. And the relation that we have is always compassionate.

The awareness of your relationship to phenomena comes to be something like that. It isn't idealistic. It isn't up there somewhere. It isn't this visionary thing. It is actually very real. You are in this sense, you could say, a child of love, because you are a child of your parents. Because of the love of the parents, the phenomena is always teaching you.

Suffering

There are various tests to which a devotee is subjected: They could be of the mind, or of the intellect, of the body and so on. A number of such tests are there. In fact, God is conducting tests all the time; every occurrence in life is a test. Every thought that crops up in the mind in itself a test to see what one's reaction will be. Hence one must be viewing everything as an opportunity to gain experience, to improve oneself and to go to a higher stage.

-Nityananda

A: It is said that in the Garden of Eden, human beings were divided from their original wholeness and harmonious relationship with the earth, with themselves and with God. And yet we seek that wholeness. There is the contradiction.

J: Do you run away from suffering or do you embrace it? Can the same person who is avoiding it, embrace it? My answer would be they can't. We say, "In time, if I work toward it, I will be over it." But, the concept of time causes more suffering. Something immediate and spontaneous has to happen for the person to actually be with it. They're not avoiding it, they're embracing it, or it's embracing them.

A: Jesus embraced suffering, or it embraced him in it's entirety on the cross, resolving it for humanity. Yet individuals still need to resolve suffering for themselves.

J: From the Buddhist or Zen standpoint, what is more important is the resolution of understanding what that is. What is suffering? We see what this suffering has caused, but is that all that we suffer from?

This is a translation from "The Heart Sutra," taken from my teacher, Seikan Hasegawa's book The Cave of Poison Grass:

> When the Bodhisattva Avalokitesvara practiced the deep Prana-paramita, he perceived that the Five Skandas are all empty, and was free from all sufferings.
>
> My Saraputra, form is no different from emptiness. Emptiness is no different from form. Form is emptiness, as itself, and emptiness is form, as itself. The same can be said of sensation, thought, volition and consciousness.
>
> My Saraputra, this empty form of all Dharmas can not be born, and not be ruined. Not be polluted, and not be purified. And not be increased, and not be decreased. Therefore in emptiness, there is not form, sensation, thought, volition and consciousness. And not eyes, nose, tongue, body and mind. And not matter, sound, smell, taste, touch and laws. And not the world of eyes,....until the world of consciousness. There is not ignorance, ...and not the end of ignorance. Until not old age and death, and not the end of old age and death; there is not suffering, accumulation, annihilation and the way. There is not wisdom and not attainment, because there is not that which can be attained.
>
> Bodhisattva has no obstacles in his mind, because he is living in the Prana-paramita; and he has no fears, because there are no obstacles. He

has gone far beyond the delusions and illusions, and perfected Nirvana.

All Buddhas of the three worlds live in Prana-paramita; therefore they get the Anuttara-samyak-sambodhi, (the unsurpassed perfect wisdom). Therefore we should know that the Prana-paramita is the great mysterious Mantram, the great wisdom Mantram, the great supreme Mantram, the great peerless Mantram, which can remove all sufferings very well; it is truth, but not falsehood. Then there is the Mantram of Prana-paramita. It said, "Gate, gate, parasamgate, bodhi, svaha!ii"

A: As I understand it, this sutra expresses the essence of Buddhist teaching. About the suffering: In Christianity, suffering and its resolution is also at the heart of the cross. It goes back to the beginning. In the Garden of Eden we understand original suffering, or "sin," as related to the state of being divided or separated from God.

The cross resolves the separation and thus resolves the suffering, at the same time without taking away the suffering which everyone has in life. There is the contradiction of the cross.

Again, someone will ask, "How is the suffering resolved?" It is resolved one challenge at a time, one test at a time. We pass through trials and then it is resolved. It is resolved by going through it, by, as you say embracing it, not by avoiding it.

As I heard your reading, it sounds as though this is also at the heart of it. There is the annihilation of suffering, yet there is a contradiction. It's suffering, but at the same time being released from it. How does Avalokitesvara take all sufferings as his, and yet be at the same time be freed from all sufferings?

J: One is free because he perceived them as "empty." Of course, suffering is always going to affect you. Particular suffering may be greater for one person, than for the other person. Suffering is there, but you take suffering and enjoyment on an equal footing.

If you crave more enjoyment, you may get it for a time, but then once it's gone, you suffer, because you no longer have it. So, people suffer in that way, not getting what they want.

A: Then in the <u>Cave of Poison Grass</u>, your teacher writes:

> In the late nineteenth century, the great Japanese general Saicho, also said, 'Unless a person doesn't care about men, money, women, death, he is not able to do any great work. However if I understand in the Mahayana way, this saying means without solving these, and graduating from these, we cannot do any great work.[iii]

He's alluding to a process of going beyond it, and yet having to go through something to get "beyond" it. It's not like you wake up and there's no suffering.

J: The term "resolve" or "graduate" from suffering are used in the sense that now you go beyond that, now you go to this next class. It's the idea of cultivating learning and getting to that point. Ten years ago I understood something one way. Ten years later I perceive it in a completely different way. Somehow it is not so much of a problem. Somehow I graduated. I came to this point.

I think there is a sense, when one hears the word "emptiness," that you blank out and depersonalize yourself. You detach, go beyond or transcend suffering. It's hard to grasp this idea about suffering in the "Heart Sutra" from a personal standpoint. It does seem that you are trying to detach yourself, while from what you were just reading, there is the human element. But, you don't try to detach from yourself. You involve yourself. You put yourself in that. You don't try to go beyond it. That is where you get that vitality, that creativity.

There still is suffering. Buddha said, "Life is suffering." He said, "We suffer because of *klesa*, because of attachment. But, our attachment is attachment to our idea of suffering. For the most part, we want to have the least amount of suffering. We don't usually invite it. Take, for example, people whose work comes from a desire to help and to share in the suffering of others, someone like Mother Theresa. While I imagine the decision to do that kind of work is out of some conviction, I doubt that the person is saying to herself or himself "Look at me, I'm suffering," or "Look how kind I am, I'm trying to make things better for this world."

A: I also see suffering in an evolutionary way. The author of the "Letter to the Hebrews" says that Jesus went through this therefore we know that endurance will be required of us. He gives examples, of Abraham and others who followed in the faith and who were "tested" along the way, having to overcome. I think that is similar to what you were saying about "resolving," or "graduating."

When you meet what comes at you in life, and you go through it, rather than avoiding it, there is a different vista that you reach on the other side of that "test." You may not be beyond suffering, but at each step you are learning more, and you are getting a little bit freer as you go along.

J: It's getting to that point of cultivating learning.

A: Yes.

"*Believe in Me*"

This talk took place at Mount Saviour monastery in Elmira, New York, another place where John had stayed over the years and where we visited. As had been the case in New Mexico, we were the only guests at the monastery. I had a lovely room at the women's lodgings, St. Gertrude's, while John stayed at the men's lodgings at the bottom of the hill. It was late spring and the rolling acreage of hills surrounding the monastery couldn't have been more beautiful. There was nothing to be seen for miles around besides the beauty of the creation. The stillness and serenity of the stay was punctuated only once by a visit into town for ice cream cones. We attended daily worship at the chapel and met up together a couple of times a day for conversation. We were sitting overlooking the hills behind St. Gertrude's when we had this talk.

A: In John's gospel, Jesus says, "The one who believes in me, will also do the works that I do and, in fact, will do greater works than these.[iv]" (14:12). How do you understand this?

J: For one's Self. I think the only way is by one's Self and for one's Self. It seems as though, in my experience, there is no one really there that has the capability to pass it on. You have to look elsewhere. One of the things that my teacher would do is quote from the Bible from time to time in his writings. He did it with me because he knew my interest in Christianity and felt that was one of the best ways to teach me about it.

A: You say one has to look elsewhere, but where is one to look?

J: From the Source. As long as we want to be told that we're bad or we're good, we'll be judged, we'll compare. Did I do good Daddy or Mummy? Did I do good God? As long as a parental relationship is there, it will be impossible to approach the Source, your Self. With or without somebody the Source is here, the Truth is here. It's ever present. But you don't shut your self off and say, "Well forget about going there, we'll just order pizza or Chinese," and have nothing to do with the outside world. It's not like that.

How can you understand the Source or Truth of your Self unless there is another one to mirror back or to bounce it back? How can we practice compassion without another? How do we know this Buddha mind, this Primordial Nature? How do we know the Supreme Reality, the Brahman? To say it's us and we are the Source may sound a very fuzzy, ephemeral, vague thing. I can understand why Christ would say, "Believe in me." It's using him as that bouncing board.

Believe what? That means to me that you simply go along with that. In going along, you're going to find that it's not easy to go along. There are bumps in the road, and these are your relationship to your Self. Internally and externally, those bumps that you encounter are all about your Self. To believe sounds good, but you can't really do that exactly. So why don't we just say, "Believe in your Self," or "Look at the Truth within?"

First, there has to be something there, an understanding from the level of having to really try and put that into practice. You have to start somewhere. Somewhere along in the line in your life, or your karmic life, something has to happen. I think it's important to really grasp what that is.

If you were to believe that you were the Source, you would be paying more attention to your Self, and all your feelings, emotions, and thoughts. Usually what we do is we take ourselves outside. We're always thinking of others and of external things that take us away from ourselves and pull us out.

A: So Jesus doesn't mean "Believe in me" as this outside person? I say this because that is how many are used to understanding it.

J: Oh, no!

A: Well, I doubt that's what the author of John's gospel intended, but I imagine that pointing to the Source within would be consistent with what Jesus intended.

God speaks to us

saying, "I became man

for you. If you do not

become God for me you

do me wrong."

-Meister Eckhart

Part Two:

On the Path

These next talks took place the following year on one of two porches on Amelia Island, Florida where John and I spent that year as neighbors. The scenery had changed. The main porch to "the Manor" (mine), and the one next door to "the Cottage" (his), as we dubbed them, were located in the historic district of an island town just south of the Georgia border and looked out over the local funeral parlor. We would meet in the mornings for coffee and conversation. Our talks would often be interrupted by the noise of logging trucks rolling up and down the main street syncopated by the sound of our dogs barking in the background. In the evenings, instead of water birds, at 6:30 p.m. we were greeted by the sight of our neighbor Felix on his tricycle selling $1 bags of boiled and regular peanuts and occasionally stopping to entertain us with a riff from his blues harmonica.

Thinking and reflecting is

what makes a person.

A true person thinks and reflects.

Ignorance of the path to the

Self leads to rebirth

Again and again.

-Nityananda

Prayer

A: Let's talk about prayer.

J: In <u>The Cloud of Unknowing</u>, a book written in England in the 14th century by an unknown author about the soul's quest for God, the author talks about using a word, preferably a one-syllable word. By focusing on that word, by having it inside of you, you pierce that cloud of unknowing, and go through. He talks about different levels of what you go through.

A: The author says, "Why does this little prayer of one syllable pierce the heavens? Surely because it is offered with a full spirit, in the height and the depth, in the length and the breadth of him who prays.[v]"

J: I think of *japa* beads, prayer beads. You can use that one syllable, *om* or *ma*, or *mu*, for each bead, chanting at first maybe outwardly, then inwardly in your mind. It becomes more and more subtle over time, and then encapsulates you. It takes you to that one condensed place and you break through that to something else.

A: The author talks about the power of this one kind of prayer, this one syllable, and how it is heard by God, and how God immediately responds no matter what the condition of the soul. Because it's "Piercing through to the height and the depth and the length and the breadth of the spirit" it is then "helped by God," the author says, in the "very vehemence of this going out." That is interesting to me.

J: Why is it interesting to you?

A: The word itself is going out and having an effect. God is responding and something is happening. The word is piercing in the "very vehemence of the going out."

J: The meaning would be in that emotional, devotional or passionate connection to what it is you are doing.

A: The meaning would be in the passion not in the words.

J: Yes, in the passion.

A: This is very important. It is different from saying words or using forms to cause a result. This single-syllable prayer can then take us outside of the realm of thought.

J: Having a *koan* or *japa*, or chanting, involves more of your body, more of your being. There is very little place to think, "maybe if I do this, this will come to me." When you're doing it, you're just doing it. You're forgetting your body, your mind, everything. Your mind is going to simply focus on this one thing and your body is included in the process. As one teacher once said, "Chanting, whether inwardly or outwardly, helps to purify the mind."

A: Do you think prayer shift us to a more Universal perspective?

J: Your life is already self-enclosing. It's about your self-centered needs wants and desires. Even if you try to work with that, and say, "Maybe I need to give a little bit of this away," or "maybe I need to not think of this so much "life still creates conditions where you think of yourself. It becomes a self-focused way of living.

If prayer is just a continuation of that, then, thinking that one is supplicating to a higher power, one might feel a bit better about their life. A person may think "I'm not getting what I want," and "maybe God will come in and take care of those needs." But it is still just from the personal basis, the place where you have been standing and moving all your life. It doesn't matter if it's God or Buddha or whomever, it's from that basis of that self-enclosed, self-centered and self-self of what I need.

A: Some people pray to transcend themselves.

J: You're saying people hope to go beyond their self-centeredness?

A: Yes and they have a picture of what that means.

J: Let's say you're feeding your dog or your cat. You are performing an act. You're not thinking about yourself in this case.

You have this animal, and you're not thinking, "If I do this, I'll feel better." In the beginning, it may feel good to have an animal that keeps you company, but day in and day out you just may not want to open that can of tuna. You may want to get a cup of coffee and sit down, and that's it. But you've got a cat and its saying, "Feed me, feed me."

You have to do this because you know this animal is very dependent on you. So, these situations in life present themselves, if you want to say, as a form of prayer.

Prayer is giving over and forgetting oneself in the act of performing. That place where you are not thinking of "I" or "me," but just the act itself.

Prayer depends on the state of mind of the person. If you're bringing all of the particular you there, that's all there is. It might seem like you're praying to God, but it's just you. The idea of what we think of as God, however one may envision that - this solid personality up there, or this fuzzy spiritual thing, or a feeling of some sort - is just simply the projection of ourselves. We can make a projection about anything we want. Like a self-hypnosis.

A: Self-hypnosis creates false reality.

J: One could say that it is a false reality, because the reality is based on one's self; on one's desires, fears and wants. We look through our own sunglasses when we create that subjective reality. In some sense the animal reality is objective reality. Subjectively you say, "Forget it. I don't want to do this." Objectively it's still there, even though your mind is saying, "I really don't want to do this." The important thing is to let go of your thoughts and let your body act and perform the motions at that time, leaving your thoughts aside. Maybe at another time your thoughts come in and your body can sit and do nothing. But if you use thoughts to dictate everything you do, you're in trouble.

You're shedding body and mind and leaving it behind. You can't think you're going to do something to shed body and mind. Somehow there is the act, like feeding the animals, that moves and takes you along. Thoughts come in of whether you want to or not but you forget about it and just go along.

Take Jesus for example. He was already in that place of Universal connection. He lived it. He breathed it. His whole life was about that. People tend to segregate and compartmentalize their lives. They say, "This prayer time is part of my religion" or, "This prayer time is part of my spiritual practice, or "This activity isn't prayer," or "I'll have that over here," or "I'll do this over there." Spirituality is then more like twenty-five percent of your life. Twenty-five percent is almost like no percent, unless that twenty-five percent grows to a larger percentage. Then increasingly your whole body, your whole mind, your actions and your behavior become a manifestation of that.

A: Say more about how a person increases that percentage.

J: In going along you're forgetting yourself, you're lessening your self-concern and your self-importance. You're simplifying the things that you feel you need or have to do. Say, you wake up one morning and you realize, "I used to do that and I used to feel the need, but I no longer do. Why is that?" It's hard to say, but something is happening.

A: Like listening to something that might direct an outer change.

J: But not as an object, but listening to your own Being.

A: Being willing to risk being changed inwardly and outwardly in our lives – In any case, the changes are being produced. It calls for a certain action on our part, a willingness to move with the change.

J: You're allowing the prayer to live through you. You say, "I'm going to pray," in whatever form that may take, but then the prayer embraces you, and that's the transforming quality.

If you don't allow anything to come into your life and give it space, no matter what it is, how can you ever change? Take someone who has been living alone all their lives. And this cat starts to visit them. They try to shoo the cat away at first, but then over time, you have the cat coming in saying "I am here and I am going to live here." It keeps returning, coming back .... And then you put out a little food and then you invite it in and the next thing you know you've formed this relationship to the cat. And it's broadened your life because you've allowed that animal to come into your life.

A: All this becomes prayer. One might look at one's resistance to that. The cat has come in and there it is, then a movement has happened in and there is the embrace. And there is the growth.

Let's talk about prayer and healing.

J: There is a movement that has created a change of circumstances, a shift of some sort. Maybe the person who has been healed was receptive at that point.

A: It can happen in different ways, through chanting, or sound as we've said, but then I was reading about an Indian sage around whom healings just unselfconsciously happened.

J: So, there is some energy or something that becomes manifest in a material way. And why at that time does that happen?

A: And is the one who makes it happen a certain kind of person, a so-called holy person, or someone who has achieved self-realization?

J: Maybe some good things have happened, but other things are still a disaster. You can wish for something very, very much and get it... As they say "Beware of what you wish for."

A: Yes, "Be careful what you pray for."

J: The thing about this, Ashley, to be really careful of, is where people feel that they are channeling other people or having conversations with God. I look at how easy it is for people to fall into trying to explain the unexplainable. I think all those books are really not good. They are all dealing with the unseen, the unmanifested, and then objectifying it. Anything objectified can be bought and sold in the spiritual marketplace.

Practice

I learned both what is secret and what is manifest, for wisdom, the fashioner of all things taught me.

There is in her, a spirit that is intelligent, holy, unique, manifold, subtle, mobile, clear, unpolluted, distinct, invulnerable, loving the good, keen, irresistible, beneficent, humane, steadfast, sure, free from anxiety, all-powerful, overseeing all and penetrating through all spirits that are intelligent, pure and altogether subtle.

For wisdom is more mobile than any motion; because of her pureness she pervades and penetrates all things. For she is the breath of the power of God, and a pure emanation of the glory of the Almighty; therefore nothing defiled gains entrance into her.

for she is a reflection of eternal light, a spotless mirror of the working of God, and an image of his goodness. Although she is but one, she can do all things, and while remaining in herself, she renews all things; in every generation she passes into holy souls and makes them friends of God and prophets....

–Wisdom of Solomon (7:21-27)[vi]

A: Realization and love must come from our real self. It would seem that heart of my practice would be to encourage that connection.

J: Yes, its understanding what is at the heart of the practice. Its fine and well to have ritual practice like prayer and chanting but the concern here is the is the connection you are really making and in order to make that connection it comes from a different approach. Now you are on your own as an individual reflecting in your own particular way.

A: At the same time it's beyond me in some sense.

J: We can't just see it from this particular way, as though spiritual life is something to be practiced and grasped. We can't think that there must be a way to attain realization through our usual means of thinking, like we attain cars, money, food or friendship.

Friendship comes from a growth, an evolution. Friendship cannot be gotten. Just as deeper or real love, as opposed to romantic love, cannot be attained or grasped but is an evolution, respect is also an evolution. Everything can teach you love and respect. We cannot learn or attain love and respect by studying a particular thing or by taking on a spiritual practice, or by reading certain things. The time that something is entering you is already past. I'm mentioning love and respect in that way. Both those things are a practice. And one learns in hindsight.

There is knowing what love is and what love is not. How do we think of love? How do we think of respect? Is it just our idea of it; or just what we want from it? Do we think the way we do just because we were told that this was the way that one should do it, or it that this is the way it should be?

This is where the awareness of your existence comes in. Your ideas of love, your resistance and the barriers that come up in you are that which divide you from yourself. There is a discernible physical sense. When you are divided, you are alienated from something. It's like when you have an argument with a friend, say, and you feel just horrible. Then you want to try to have an understanding of that person. I think, in that same way, if we divide our daily life into something else that we think we should practice, we're missing the point.

A: Yes, right.

J: It is like a circle coming around. You hear things sometimes that make sense and you say, "Yes I've heard that before." But you can come around it again and understand a little bit more about it. You hear it in a different way, in a different context. That is the real meaning of practice or training. You're growing in that understanding. You aren't just saying, "Well okay, now I've got it and that's it." You know?

A: You're getting it at a different level.

J: You're getting it at a different level all the time and the awareness that comes in is of something that is more reflective in you. There is a reflection in you that becomes a little bit more acute. It's not like "Here today gone tomorrow," like a falling star disappearing into blackness. What you come to understand now reflects itself more brightly in you.

A: The meaning of reflection changes.

J: Most likely something hasn't impacted you that much if you're only thinking from the head. Or else, what's happened is that it's hit you and you've tried to remove yourself feeling-wise from it and then it's gone. You're trying to think it through at your head level and it's dispersed. It doesn't have the impact it had before. In other words, something happens because it had an impact on you and you are choosing to avoid it, internally or externally, by busying yourself, or calling a friend or whatever.

Bodhidharma says that there are two ways to enter understanding, or to understand the way. One is through reason and the other is through practice. Through reason we are able to see and understand the basic equality and innate nature of all beings. It is not just reasoning but being able to put things into practice. It's like letting go. Letting go means not insisting on your way, viewpoint or usual interpretation of things. There are things you can tell yourself, for example not to give value judgments. Who is giving value judgments to others? One's body, this Buddha nature, is completely one substance and not fragmented. That's why Bodhidharma says to firmly believe in the innate equality of all beings - being the same substance, the same nature, no difference.

Practicing, by not giving value judgments, is to remind oneself to "Love thy enemy." To remind one's self and deepen one's understanding, that this person is no different than me. When you come up against the limitation of your understanding, you see that you can move ahead a little bit further. But if you are insisting on your own viewpoint and always seeing the differences when they arise, then it's hard to move ahead.

Intelligence is also the strength of your practice. If you go to a church or a group and talk about your problems, you may feel better momentarily, but you don't go away with that much intelligence. You're not bringing it into that much wider scope especially if there is nobody there that has the insight to bring it out and strengthen it. It helps to talk about your feelings and it can be useful to get them out and that can help you realize something. But, what has given me great strength and growth of awareness, Ashley, is when I bring that to the Universal, to a much wider scope. Then that feeds me. Before it was particular, worldly John who had worked something out and felt better, but then when I move it out to the Universal...John, so to speak, it puts me in alignment to something, and that alignment makes me realize that this is really the important thing.

43

A: What do you mean when you say you "bring that to the Universal?"

J: An example would be instead of following your first thought of how you would handle something, to not act, but to just let it lie, let it rest. Take your mind, thoughts and feelings off of it and just relax. In relaxing one may be surprised that something else may come up. It would be the Universal that would be coming up. It has come to you. When I say "moving" it's more like moving out of your own way, stepping aside.

Inner wisdom is also part of practice. This wisdom. comes from you, and I'm not speaking of a personal me, but Life, your origin. We call *prana*, vital breath, that manifests itself in all beings. We could say, it has emerged of itself, in a more physical place. There is more of a "physical" rather than an intellectual one. And then one could call that Buddha Nature. That's when wisdom shows itself and begins to speak to you directly.

Knowing the Self

A: It's difficult to talk about knowing the Self.

J: We are educated to know how to do math, to work at a job or to perform certain functions in life. Knowing becomes the "knowing" of something else, as an object. But, when you hear the words, "knowing your Self," it brings it back to you and not any other person or object. It is of value to reflect deeply on these words. In that way you're shifting the position where you normally are, to a position where you normally are not.

A: I would study a subject objectively. You are saying this is a different kind of study and knowledge.

J: You could take the Self as an object distinct from yourself in your mind, but you're shifting your position to something which is moving, which is hard to catch. We could say when you learn something, you learn through your senses. You see it or hear it, for example. But this is not like looking at your hand and thinking, "If I look at my hand, or hear my hands clapping, I'm going to learn something." I might train myself, say on the guitar, and watch and use my fingers to go up and down, as we know. After a period of practice, you get better. But this Self, what is this Self, we're talking about? Is this Self just a mere body?

I'm saying it is not. What you see in the body is a mechanical apparatus. Inside, you can't really see what is going on. You may feel, sense or intuit some things that are going on inside. Such as when you get a stomachache you might sense something is going on before you get a full-blown stomachache. That is using your awareness to learn about this body. But I am saying that the Self is not just the body.

So, we could say we've moved into the mind. That becomes more of a moveable, changeable, elusive thing. We know in our everyday life, if we are at least somewhat attentive, that we see things about ourselves from the things that we do. It's always in relationship to something-to a person, to your animal, to something that you're doing or thinking about. Like waves, it becomes much more moveable. You are then, looking at these waves made up of thoughts, emotions and feelings.

We could say that coming to know the Self is the Self of the body and the Self of the mind. In the mind it is predominately our thoughts and feelings, what moves and motivates us, or what creates an action. If we have a certain belief, we'll act according to that belief. The person next to us will act according to their belief. They could have the same beliefs, or opposite beliefs. But you're aware of yourself. Everything in that range makes up you. And as you become aware of your neighbor, if you get to know them better you become more aware of them. But just that statement "knowing your Self" has a stilling effect. It stops you. It's saying "Stop looking outward. Now, start looking inward. Start looking at what is going on in oneself." So, you could say the object of the task is your Self. We could say scientifically that, "John is knowing John. John is learning about John."

A: It sounds like you're talking about the ego-bound self? What is the importance of this study?

J: If we're going to die anyway?

A: Yes. Or, why study the ego?

J: That depends on what is at the bottom of your mind. If you take that attitude I would say, "There is something fatalistic about this person. They must not be too happy. They must be a little depressed, sad, angry maybe.

A: Maybe philosophical.

J: To enter into philosophical debate with oneself is, in my opinion, a waste of time. What is the value of philosophizing about knowing your Self if it has no basis in reality, if it has no basis in your actual body? Is it just ghost-like? That has no value except for entertainment and mind games.

Really you love your Self. I don't mean romantic or emotional love. This is love that reaches beyond relative love. This love is continually present. The presence of your very Being is the expression of this love.

A: If I could answer my own question, "What is the purpose of studying the Self?" I would say, the purpose is life and love itself.

J: Yes.

A: Life and love cause our growth and learning. We respond to that which comes into our lives by studying it.

People are constantly encouraged to look elsewhere for meaning, to imaginary realms, religious systems and the stories and myths that we have created. The myths themselves help to interpret reality, but cannot replace it. Sometimes we latch onto the myths as if they were reality itself, thereby avoiding reality. In this way we avoid our own lives, our own selves, and we avoid coming to know the Self. Then, in a sense, we have missed the point.

But I think we are in a depressed culture and that depression and anger are symptoms of something that needs to be changed. There is something that we do not understand.

J: That's right.

A: We reach out to fill our needs externally and it doesn't work. Then we become depressed. I think that letting go of our illusions also contributes to the sadness.

J: In that sense we can learn about ourselves by what we see in the social world. I heard one meaning of religion as "the discipline to know." That makes a lot of sense. If that is the interpretation of it, then we've gotten off track from that.

A: In the heart of every person is the desire, I think, to make contact with the Self, with that which is Real. We want our lives to mean something. We don't want to go through life in a dull haze. We want passion. How do we make a start in another direction?

J: Realizing that something is wrong is an important starting point. It is important that you begin to see what it is not. Don't immediately try to find quick answers or resolutions by going from person to person or teaching to teaching. Stay with your Self to discover for yourself, and ultimately by yourself.

When you realize something is amiss and not connecting somehow, when you really get that, then I'm assuming a wish arises to have Self-realization, to know something more or to connect with something larger. That desire motivates your outward and inward action, though here I'm mainly talking about the inward action. That wish is very important because it is, if I could say, equal to faith. The wish now moves out from your Self individually. Whether you know it or not, that wish is now moving out to a larger space, embracing and encompassing more.

It's the physical feeling that you get, the sensation of this opening up. It's the opening up that I'm trying to relate to. When that wish is truly felt, truly from your gut, from your heart, then that is the moving out and, as I see it that is the faith.

It is faith because you don't know exactly where it is going. There is no particular point that you're moving that out to. You're not moving it out to a church, or a person, or a group. You're just moving out. The wish that exists in and of its self, which is so strong, which is so heartfelt, goes out. And that wish is the beginning.

We're not talking about, "I want less stress," or "I wish I could do this," or "I wish God would come into my life," or "I wish I would have this or that..." or "I wish that people would be more loving." It's not that kind of wish. That's your personal wish, coming only from your ego. This other wish is a wish that moves out from the Self.

That is the beginning and that is also the continuation. That is the development, the growth and the practice, but not in the sense of trying to practice in a certain form. Sometimes it happens that when people have a very strong wish they move in a direction, but they move into a structured environment that can confine that initial desire. Like a young person who has a strong desire to help the world. They get out in the world and realize it's a different story. It is the same for a person at any age that begins with that initial wish, and then realizes that the world is not necessarily responding to it.

That is when we move into the area of faith, because it takes faith as well as courage to continue and sustain that wish. When that wish is supported and encouraged it's like keeping the fire burning. Never let that diminish. It doesn't matter what age you are as long as you keep that fire going.

A: How can we keep that fire burning?

J: Keep reminding yourself mentally that you are much, much more than what you think you are.

A: We've said we need someone to support and encourage us. As I understand it, one of the purposes of a good teacher is to help cut away the ego so that this bigger dimension can emerge.

J: Even though you have had that initial wish, the ego and your personal views and concepts are continually catching you up...tripping you in the hallway. Your own personal way of looking at things still comes out. It becomes mixed in and convoluted. That's why using your mind as a tool to be clear and honest about things is very important and, yes, a teacher is there to remind you of that and to remind you of that essential nature that you are.

A: Can a person realize themselves without a teacher?

J: People would like to think so. People would like to realize and do a lot of things by themselves. I'm also not saying to run out and get a teacher. I don't see that so much as a question to say, "Now I've decided that I'm not going to have a teacher, because I'm going to do it on my own," or "Now I've decided I will have a teacher." That's like someone saying, "Now I've decided I'm a Baptist." They want to define, confine, box in and feel secure and okay. You're already setting up your own conceptual framework of how you're going to deal with reality. You say, "I'm not going to have a teacher," so you've boxed yourself in.

Something or somebody may come along. I think life brings you what it needs to bring you. Even if life brings you something that may be somewhat disastrous, it's there also to teach you something. Hopefully at every turn, at every corner, you're learning something.

A: So just stay with the point of desire then....

J: Yes, stay with the desire, stay with the wish- that is Love. Love is that innate connection to everything. When you're in that place you're open to many possibilities. Then you begin to truly flow. Then you lessen or cut away from your own value judgments and prejudices and you begin to embrace this world more as a whole, rather than pieces of a whole.

A: You begin to see the things that are coming in as helpful to your wish, whether you might have previously considered them "good" or "bad," or to be avoided.

J: Right. In this sense everything becomes Buddha, everything becomes God. You aren't saying "Well this thing over here is nasty, I mustn't go there." Whether it's nasty or beautiful, now it's seen in its basic equality. Take away the nasty then it's just Buddha. Nasty God, beautiful God, just God now.

A: Both there to free up Love.

J: That's right. So, there could be value, say, in an outward practice of doing something that you are reluctant to face or approach. Now you might begin to approach that even though you feel resistance physically. Face your resistance, not pushing it away but saying, "I see you resistance, I see you fear. Okay, that's fine, you're here. In the meantime, if it's okay with you I'm going to go ahead with this;" gently, calmly and not forcefully. In that outward action there is an opening up.

I don't mean that if I have a fear of heights I'm going Bunji jumping. It has nothing to do with that. That is just your personal thing. I'm talking about something different from climbing the Himalayas. It might be something as simple as communicating with your neighbor.

A: As you said it's becoming Buddha.

J: Right, your practice is the practice of Buddha; your practice is the practice of God. If I was to say to you, "You are Buddha," what does that mean? Well it means act like Buddha. Be Buddha. Don't be Ashley or John or Frank or the usual self that says, "Well I'm going to get out there and I'm going to do this thing, and I'm going to achieve...." Go out get a job. Do this. Do that. Follow your ambitions. This world of Buddha or God is from a different place - it's from a place that you are manifesting Buddha, you're showing up as Buddha, not as this other personal self.

Of course you have to remind yourself of that because you forget. It doesn't mean you walk around going "I am Buddha, I am Buddha, I am Buddha," like a mantra. May be you might do that for a little while but....

A: I would remind myself often because I forget.

J: The reminding is in itself the creation of that wish again.

A: It gets back to trusting life and hanging on to that desire.

J: Of course that wish, that desire, is fluid, sometimes slippery. Just shine, shine brightly.

Life –Death

A: What do you think happens when we die?

J: Probably not much. Dying is completely dying, and we don't need to add anything onto that.

A: Religions talk about what happen to people after they die. I don't think we can ignore the question.

J: Dead is dead. Death is complete. Absolute time, not divided, not separate. At the same time, I remember once asking my Zen teacher the question, "What happens afterwards?" He said, "We continue training." He said that there is continued practice and training. Does that mean that we become this other entity and that we're going to find ourselves in the mountains again or go to another planet? Who truly knows? I think the present is more important to resolve. To resolve death, resolve life. Understand really who you are here and now.

A: Jesus said the "Kingdom of God is among you." (Luke 17:21). There is no other time than the present.

J: We give continuation to things by our memory, by our thinking. That makes us think we're living at this point and then later we'll die.

A: We identify with the body.

J: We identify with our body and our thoughts. We are truly a body. We create a space in which we identify that our body moves around and does what it does. This makes up our idea of "me," of who I am.

A: But these bodies are actually an expression of something.

J: Yes, but what we're saying is that our perception stops with the body and with the identification with the thought. That becomes the place in which we see who we think we are.

A: I see. About life after death though; Christians claim particularity of the person. The resurrection event points to this. As the story is told, there is continuity between Jesus' resurrection appearances and his person - not his physical person, but his personality it would seem. Sometimes he appeared looking as he had before his death, such as when he appeared with the marks of the crucifixion and was recognizable to the disciples. In another place, he appears as the gardener, and it's up to Mary to discover who he is. At another time he appears to a couple of disciples in Jerusalem, as a stranger. Through his conversation with them they recognize him. There is a sense in which at a spiritual level, that person is still recognizable as who they were. They might not look physically the same; yet, there is the recognition. I think that implies that there is a particularity of person, however we define that.

J: We identify ourselves with our bodies, our thoughts and emotions. When that goes, everything goes. But then there is the questioning of who one is. When that inquiry begins to take place, one begins to doubt the way they have seen and thought of themselves, of other people and of the world.

It would be quick and evasive to say that when we die we go back into the Absolute, or we go back to God, when in actuality, apparently there is that very Absolute, Ultimate Reality present here and now, and not necessarily to be looked for elsewhere, because there is only the here and now.

A: After I die, what, would you say, is my relationship with the Absolute, with God?

J: Well, I would say that it's never separate. It's thinking that makes us feel we are separate.

A: One early Christian used the image of the sun. The sun is one, and yet has rays. These souls or these expressions of the Divinity are as rays. They are distinctive and yet not separate from the sun.

J: That's a great image. Each person is unique and is not separate from the very sun that it is absolutely connected to.

A: Let's go back to what your teacher said about what happens to us after we die.

J: In life after life, you are continuing on. You continue training and practicing. That's saying of course that it's not the end of something, that there is a continuation. If my life is only filled up with social worldly things, then reasoning and looking at it logically, I also realize that my going to the church or temple was just an extension of the social worldly mannerisms. Let's take a simple example. If all a person ever did was live in the social world, maybe did some bad things in his life, and didn't do much, then what happens when he dies? It seems to me that there was an opportunity in their human life to do something and it never happened. Something must happen. For that person there is no continued practice, no continued training, no continued growth and learning. Maybe we could say that person continues on in the same place or maybe goes backwards or downward rather than upward. Maybe some people would think, "This person's fine, because they went to church and repented and so forth."

When I look at people, I look at life. As I know and study life more and more, I am also studying death. That is why I say that some people can only go backwards, because they are only going backwards or stagnating in their life. Stagnating is the same thing as going backwards. There is no going forward.

A: People go backwards because they haven't used their life in the proper way or they are dragging their attachments with them.

J: Attachment to things is really attachment to the illusion of self. It doesn't matter whether you have fifteen Mercedes cars, or whatever else you have, the attachment is attachment to the illusion of yourself. I do think that there is the relative -the higher and lower. It seems that for those that have evolved there is only the higher and for those that have not evolved there is only the lower. Lower in the sense that maybe they have to repeat, go through or maybe even drop out.

There are people who think there is energy and that we go off and that there is space and that space will get mixed in with space. We know that this is not real. When there is no you, there is no consciousness. And therefore there is no God. As Nisargadatta would say, "If there is no consciousness, there is no God." There is nothing. You're not around. Like space being space.

Maybe we think there's this energy material and we're going to pluck it out and say, "Okay, you're over here," or something like that. It must be more like riding a wave. In that way there is a flow, and in that flow maybe there is a direction and somehow something came out. Something came out of that space, emptiness is form, and here we are.

A: Right.

J: We're not just space. We are physical consciousness, but we came here, there is something here. The idea that we have of ourselves is not real. But we are relatively real.

When I think of energy, I think of filling space. Energy is filling space. If you take away that house there, there will be air made up of molecules and different things. We can see spaciousness, the air and all that is still going on. When we use the word space, is space like that? Or, is it space where there are no molecules, no nothing? Silence is space as I see it.

A: I see.

J: We could say that there is something in that silence. Maybe some other type of sound. So there are both. There is both space and non-space.

A: Even if we're not here in our physicality that doesn't mean that we've gone elsewhere.

J: You think of some of the great sages of India. When they die they still have an effecting power. It comes in the form of actually seeing them or in the form of dreams or something happening just when they die. What is that? It is something like the world or the phenomena working with that person in alignment with that energy.

A: What about people who have had near death-experiences and say they come back changed by them?

J: It's just phenomena. They die. They come back.

A: Less self-centered, with a wider consciousness and a better sense of their purpose on earth apparently.

J: Life and even near death can change you, just as much as an illness can change you.

A: There's a rumor that things in the afterlife are felt more acutely. It gives meaning to resolving our attachments in this life.

J: That's what I mean. There is something substantial here to work with. It is your life. Even the life of near-death is still your life coming back to have a realization, which now you have another chance to put into practice. But it's not like there is anything deeply profound about that. People may come back and have more goodness about them and be a little bit less self-centered. In other words maybe they are a little bit better than they were before. Maybe they were disastrous before, and now they're less disastrous and more of a good person.

What I hear about people who have come back is that there isn't really any profound intelligence, such as the kind that is found in the sages in India that we were talking about. It's like someone who sees a UFO. It's another phenomenon that can affect people, but it doesn't necessarily make them more intelligent. It can create a shift in their lives, but from that perspective it would be better if there was a really good basis or platform to build on. The same thing can happen in therapy, where a person has been in misery and a good therapist can have an effect and something happens. This happened to me working as a therapist. You don't even know you're having this effect, but you would look at a person and you could see that something had shifted.

But when we become less self-centered in our behavior it's more like we are making adjustments to our personality and character. Of course there's no way of gauging or measuring the degree. Maybe you were a terrible person and overnight, (didn't this happen to St. Paul?), something dramatic happened. We could say in this way that we are *en route* to a higher understanding.

What we're saying here is that it is more important to look at your upbringing, at how you behave, at your actions. That's awareness in a nutshell. Things happen. Whether you see a UFO, whether you die or come back, whether you have some horrible disease and survive it, or work through certain bad relationships, you realize something about yourself. These are important platforms. They are ways of moving on.

It's still within the phenomena; where in the phenomena is the substance, and in the substance is an awakening, an awareness. But there is more than just realizing, "Well, I'm not going to be a selfish person," or "I'm going to relax and not be so intense when I'm with other people," that kind of thing. That doesn't mean in and of itself that is going to also help you. We have to be careful because then we're almost talking about a code of living. There is more than that.

A: Outward actions....

J: Yes, outward actions and the Ten Commandments or Precepts or something that is given to you, where if you just follow these things, you'll be fine.

Let me read you this short writing by Dogen that was translated by my teacher, Rev. Seikan Hasegawa. It's called the *Shobogenzo: Shoji*, which means "Life-Death."

> When there is Buddha in life-death, there is no life-death. It is also said when there is no Buddha in life-death we are not deluded in life-death. These are the words of two Zen teachers Jiashan and Changshan respectively. They are the words of persons who have attained the Way; you certainly should not treat them carelessly. One who wishes to graduate from life-death should clarify their very meaning.
>
> Seeking Buddha outside life-death is like proceeding southward while the cart shaft points north, or like searching for the North Star in the southern sky. In such a manner one gathers more causes of life-death and strays farther from the way of freedom from bondage.
>
> Just recognize that life-death is Nirvana and that there is nothing to detest in life-death and

nothing to wish for in Nirvana. Then for the first time you are qualified to graduate from life-death.

It is false to assume that life turns to death. Life is the rank of a certain time wherein there is a past and future. Hence, in Buddha's Dharma, life is non-life. Ruin too is the rank of a certain time, wherein there is a past and a future. Hence, ruin is non-ruin. When we say life, there is nothing but life. When we say ruin, there is nothing but ruin. Therefore when life comes, it is only life; when ruin comes, do not say you must resist ruin, do not resist or wish for ruin.

This life-death is the venerable life of Buddha. If you detest and attempt to abandon it, you are nullifying the venerable life of Buddha. On the other hand, if you stick on the point that life-death is the venerable life of Buddha, and cling to it, you again are nullifying the life of Buddha, because you are keeping the figure of Buddha. If you neither dislike life-death, nor cling to life-death, for the first time you can enter the mind of Buddha. Do not judge by your thought or express with words.

Just free and forget your body and mind. Cast them into Buddha's house and let Buddha act. Follow his acts. Then with no use of force, with no consumption of your mind, you will graduate from life-death and become Buddha. Who would be stagnated in their mind?

There is one easiest way to become Buddha: Do no evil, do not attach to life-death, be compassionate of all creatures, respect upward, regard downward, do not dislike anything, do not wish for anything, have no thoughts, do not worry – this is called Buddha: seek nothing else.

Part Three

Endings & Beginnings

While we saw each other a couple of times in the interim, it would be eighteen months before we met again to wrap up these talks. By then John had moved to St. Augustine, Florida. It was there that we met on a cloudy day in January, three years after we'd first sat down together.

By now I had a new addition to the family, my boxer puppy Hildegard. She enjoyed our little road trip over on the ferry and down the Atlantic coast road that morning and stood by as my patient companion while John and I worked.

We met for Mexican food at a local restaurant on the main street, San Marco. After lunch we strolled through the grounds of a little park near St. Michael's Roman Catholic Church. This church, I was told at the bookstore, was named by Pope John Paul II as the first shrine to St. Mary during the Jubilee in 2000 and attracts many visitors.

Behind the church, nestled amongst the trees, is a tiny and beautiful ivy covered chapel called the Hermitage of Our Lady of La Leche. The sign in front informs pilgrims that the devotion to this patroness of mothers-to-be was originally brought from Spain in 1603. The chapel itself, first built in 1615, has been victim three times to war, pirates and storms.

It was here, surrounded by the past hopes and desires of visiting pilgrims, expressed through the flickers of the votive candles that bordered the chapel walls, that we sat for the final talk of this book. Later, when newly arrived visitors sought to pray where we were, we retired to the nearby gazebo with it's statue of St. Joseph, and continued to talk while watching a couple of baby squirrels playing tag among the winter leaves.

Realizing the Self

A: What do you mean by Self-realization and how do you understand it?

J: I understand Self-realization as changes which come about and things you become acutely aware of. You are realizing something for your Self.

A: In a conversation with Maharaj Nisargadatta in I Am That called "Reality Cannot be Expressed," he says to the questioner, "Anything that implies a continuity, a sequence, a passing from stage to stage cannot be real. There is no progress in reality, it is final, perfect, unrelated.... Reality is not the result of a process; it is an explosion. [vii]" We've been talking about spiritual practice and progress. Most of us think in terms of a process.

J: When you are realizing at least that you could do this instead of that or that you might not do things in the way you have done them before, you are realizing something and there is Self-realization. When you are realizing, there is the point that you make that change. Nisargadatta is talking about not defining your Self by your history.

A: Yes, he says to the questioner, "The self is single. You are that self and you have ideas of what you have been or will be. But an idea is not the self. [viii]"

J: It's something that is still there, but it's not there. It's obliterated in a sense. You're not necessarily moved by events and circumstances. When we are moved and shifted, going through emotions and thoughts it is because of how we have dealt with and been exposed to things in the past.

A: But is this question of who we are for both Maharaj and in Buddhist practice, the question that we pursue to realize the Self, a different starting point from the study of the mind?

J: All things that come into being are never avoided and never negated. If we think of spirituality as transcending or negating something, then we're really missing the point.

A: My sense is that you are embracing both viewpoints. You are saying to continually study life and yourself because all has meaning and importance. You are bringing these together. This is a very important point in these talks. To know that we should be pursuing the question of who we are, but also to know that we are here in this life and that our learning and growth from the study of this life is most important.

J: We have, to use one of my teacher's expressions, "Our warm bloody life" and that's real.

A: At the beginning of the book there is a quote about "Only he who while fully recognizing and understanding his Western heritage, penetrates and absorbs the heritage of the East, can gain the highest values of both worlds and do justice to them."

I was talking about the struggle I have had in these talks to grasp your non-dual perspective on things, coming as I have, from my own Christian training which has been from that Western dualistic viewpoint. In other words, my perception divided subject and object, me and you, inner and outer. I was not able to see, as Maharaj put it to one questioner, that I wasn't in the world the world was in me. I wasn't able to actually see the basic unity and equality of things, the emptiness of the form. These were just intellectual ideas to me during much of our talks, they were not real in my experience yet.

But later they came to be more real and in thinking about the question of Self-realization and the different ways, different paths to Self-realization, I began to question, "Is there a non-dual Christian path to Self-realization and if so is there a non-dual way to look at some of the traditional teachings of the church?" I can't go into all of those in one talk, but I started to think about just a few.

I am a woman who has been on the Christian path for my whole life. At this point, I don't wish to start on a different pathway. I have asked myself, "Can I seek Self-realization and still remain on my path?"

J: And what have you found out?

A: Maybe. I was interested to see that Stephen Jourdain[ix], the Frenchman who had an awakening when he was sixteen, has a view that is both Christian and Zen despite the fact that he was raised an atheist. Then there was Meister Eckhart, for example, who had some fairly non-dual insights. It surely is a contemplative way though.

These talks have changed my understanding of things, and I want to talk about this. How does a non-dual perspective affect certain Christian teachings? And I also want to ask a bit more about your experience.

The first point is the teaching about the image of God. This is the teaching that says that human beings are made in the image of God.

Now, let's ask, who is God? And if we can answer that, can we then, based on this teaching of imago Dei, answer the question "Who are we?" For this, after all, is the really important question.

I look in the Judeo-Christian Scriptures to a place where God actually says who he is. That is in the scene in Exodus where Moses is tending the flock of his father-in-law, Jethro and the Lord speaks to Moses out of the burning bush and tells him that he wants him to go to the Israelites and free them from bondage. And Moses says, "But if I come to the Israelites and tell them the God of your ancestors has sent me to you, 'and they ask me, 'What is his name[x]?' what shall I say to them?" Do you remember what God says to Moses?

J: "I AM WHO I AM."

A: Right, he says, "Tell them I AM sent you." So, God, and this is the only place I can think of where this happens, self-designates "I AM," A name that says what it is. And that is exactly what the Hebrew naming did. It defined the essence of the person. Naming wasn't giving a label or a symbol as it does in English. In Hebrew it was denoting the very essence of the person. So 'I AM' is the essence of God.

Now, if I am made in the image of God, what is my essence? I found it interesting in reading Maharaj Nisargadatta, to find this:

> **Q:** What did he (your guru) tell you?
>
> **M:** He told me I am the Supreme Reality.
>
> **Q:** What did you do about it?
>
> **M:** I trusted him and remembered it.
>
> **Q:** Is that all?
>
> **M:** Yes. I remembered him; I remembered what he said.
>
> **Q:** You mean to say that was enough?
>
> **M:** What more needs to be done? It was quite a lot to remember the Guru and his words. My advice to you is even less difficult than this ⬜just remember yourself. 'I am', is enough to heal your mind and take you beyond:[xi]

He's speaking of the fact that he learned from his Guru to go beyond the mind, where he found himself as the "Supreme Reality." Hence the title of the book, I Am That.

So it is this "I Am" that is my essence, that I seek to realize. Form is emptiness and emptiness is form and so I am made in the image of God. The "I Am" of God is mirrored in the "I Am" of the human.

J: Yes, one could say, the wisdom to know the emptiness and the compassion to know that you are everything, in the sense of form. In compassion you partake of everything. You relate to everything. In wisdom, you don't identify yourself as that being that you are in form. You're more than just what is there in form.

When I hear you talk about both Moses and Nisargadatta, they both trusted what was said to them. That is a very important point. The words that they heard from each, Nisargadatta from his guru, and Moses from God were the same words that were essentially already latent in them. All that was needed was like an opening of the cork in a wine bottle, to let the wine come out. Otherwise if there wasn't that merging with the person and the Absolute and God with the person, then there would be no way there could be any change or any understanding of what was being said.

A: It took him three years or something? (To achieve Self-realization.)

J: Nisargadatta?

A: Yes.

J: Something like that. I'm not exactly sure, but it did not take him that long.

A: How long did it take you?

J: Well, I would say that I understood it as time went on I guess one could say in a gradual way. Then I started to really understand the words and the teachings. I went back and forth with my own study of Christianity having come from a Christian background and later on studied Buddhism and other religions. The more I studied, the more I understood things at a deeper level. Then I could immediately see things when they were said to me with less of an obstacle.

So, I would say, at first there is the opening up to saying, "Yes, there's something I need to understand." Then there's the process of the understanding and the studying. And as you're studying too, you're putting that into practice in your life. Buddhism talks a lot about practice.

The more I was doing that, the more I was finding myself to be more than what I thought I was not just this limited human being that saw things from a personal way or from how I was brought up There was more to me now than what I had thought. And that relationship to God or Buddha became clearer.

So there was a clarity of the mind, and also the purity and opening up of the heart: Both working together. And not giving up. When I face difficulties or problems in life, I can learn and identify what it is and also learn to let go of it. And also learn to know that I'm more than that. I'm beyond that.

A: People talk about the "realized" man or woman. At the same time we talk about the training continuing. And we talk about the non-attainment of it. So, there is a paradox.

J: Well, in truth what I see as Self-realization is the saying; "Be still and know that I am God." Being still. Realizing, to use a Buddhist saying, what is your "true nature." As long as you're preoccupied, as long as you're busy in your mind, in your emotions, then you can never get to that point of knowing more of your true nature.

So, there's got to be somewhere where you just stop. You come to a point where thoughts and emotions don't run you as much as they did. But when I say, "let go and be still," there's usually some idea of effort, and I don't mean to make an effort of it. But I do think that there's a spontaneous occurrence. Some situations call for a doing and some for a non-doing. Some situations call for an effort and some for a non-effort. You're hungry. Go eat. If you're not hungry and somebody invites you out to lunch don't feel you've got to eat a big buffet meal. We could speak in that way of the little self-realizations of self-realizing, of your realizing and being able to let go of things. I think to let go, you first have to know, in a sense, what it is you're letting go of. First just understand what it is, and the letting go will take care of itself. Understand more and more what it is and things will take care of themselves.

A: So, we're trying to get to that "no-mind." Or, not trying to, but the "no-mind" place.

J: Yes, there is a "no-mind," meaning in this sense, thought-free.

A: Yes.

J: That you are not run by the mind. You are not run by thoughts, or just by the intellect or emotions. But you are actually in a position to be aware of all these things. To know that you are aware is that place of looking at yourself and knowing, because of the fact that I am aware, I am. Because I am, everything occurs. This I am is the awareness itself without having to do anything. Without having to identify itself. Just I am. You are. Awareness. Like that.

A: That's very good. Yes, this awareness is who I am. You are. Thank you.

Now I would like to go on to my second point. The second Christian teaching that I wanted to try to look at from a non-dual perspective and to ask how it relates to Self-realization is the resurrection.

Your teacher, Seikan, if I may call him Seikan, makes an interesting interpretation of the resurrection in his book. He says:

> "In my belief the Resurrection of Christ occurred when he died on the Cross, not later. When I think that both happened at once, the meaning of the Cross becomes really important to our daily life, instead of mysterious and symbolic."[xii]

I see this understanding best expressed in St. Paul's letter to the Philippians in the passage where he earlier tells the Philippians to be of one mind.

> "Let the same mind be in you that was in Christ Jesus,
> who, though he was in the form
> > of God,
> did not regard equality with
> > God
> As something to be exploited,
> but emptied himself,
> > taking the form of a slave,
> > being born in human likeness,
> And being found in human form,
> He humbled himself
> And became obedient to the
> > point of death-
> even death on a cross.
>
> Therefore God also highly
> > exalted him
> and gave him the name
> that is above every name,
> so that at the name of Jesus

68

every knee should bend,
in heaven and on earth and
under the earth,
and every tongue should
confess that Jesus Christ is Lord,
to the glory of God the Father.(2:5-9)[xiii]

It is believed that this is an early hymn. It expresses, it is called in Greek, the *kenosis*...

J: Oh, yes, yes, right...

A: ...the self-emptying. The self-emptying which, the moment of the surrender, of the death on the cross, is the moment also of the resurrection, the fullness of that God-life. It is that which, and this is where I'm asking you to help me, because I see here this movement which is part of the movement that is to happen in our realizing of Self.

J: What do you mean by movement?

A: I don't know how else to say it. In the surrender of death, in the exhalation of the human, that God- life, that resurrection life comes in. So, as you were saying earlier, in the no-mind state, in that state where the thoughts then recede, the no-mind comes in. It's similar. I'm using the word "movement" because I don't know what else to call it.

J: There's the inhalation and the exhalation.

A: I'm trying to find words for something that I'm not able to describe. To my way of thinking there's a movement.

J: I would think the movement is the movement of our ongoing life and the movement of our ongoing death- all that is close at hand. It isn't distanced. It isn't separate. Where is heaven? Is heaven up there? Is heaven separate? Or is heaven here at this moment? Is hell there somewhere? Or is hell here? I think life and death are here right now at this moment. Then it is a very real thing. It pertains to yourself right now, rather than something that you think happens down the road or something in some sort of imaginary way.

In a very blunt way, when I hear you reading St. Paul, it's like living and dying by the concept. And I don't mean just an idea of something. Here you have something that is essentially ungraspable, but yet you feel so strong, so connected with that.

Maybe other people would say, '"Well, what is this God? What is this Absolute? What is this Buddha? Does it pay my bills? "Does it buy my groceries? Will it give me a better car? No. Nothing. You get nothing from it. Yet somebody like Christ, in a sense, lived and died by the concept, to put it in a very blunt way. And how many people really live and die by the concept?

A: But surely it also means living and dying by the practical ways also. Like living and dying when the heating bill comes in and you haven't money to pay for your children's food. I mean the little things, you know, the little ways of surrendering in hopefulness that all will be well. To me that is also the practical expression of the Cross.

J: Of course we're talking at this level of someone who has completely given their life to something. They're not worrying about their heating bill so much. It doesn't mean that there may not be...

A: ...we're going to the extreme of the person who has surrendered their whole life, but there are other degrees of that.

J: Well, you could say this. You get bills for your shelter, but then you get sent a credit card with a $2,000 limit and you spend $2,000 on the credit card, but you don't have $2,000. What you need to do, is take care of your bills. So you have to let go of the idea that you need something right now. You need that new dress, those new shoes, that jewelry.

A: For everyone the learning will be at the level where they find themselves.

J: Right. And Seikan is making the point that life is a contradiction. Essentially we're finding the harmony in the balance of the contradiction. So there's the vertical and the horizontal of the cross and that place where they meet in the center. And finding that center is the important thing.

A: Good. Now, I'd like to move on to my third and last point. The teaching of the Church is a little unclear on this point as scholars are not sure what Jesus meant when he told his disciples that he would come again, but we do have the doctrine of the Second Coming of Christ. This has been especially in the public consciousness with the new millennium. Various popular books have been written and theories abound.

I have my own theory and it is not original to my thinking. It is not the usual understanding, but it is a non-dual perspective and it doesn't rely on the coming of God as an individual man a second time.

I take my understanding of the Second Coming of Christ largely from the work of Carl Jung. I believe he mentions this in his book Aion. I wonder if you've read that book.

J: I did read it many years ago, but I don't remember it very well.

A: As I understand it, Jung saw the Coming of Christ to represent the coming of the Self. He understood that this was an event that was to begin to happen in our age, though I believe he thought it would take some time for humanity to actually realize. He had some visions about things that he foresaw happening in the world of these days, not all pleasant. The main point was that he felt that the repressed contents of the psyche, several hundred year's worth, were going to be regurgitating on the world scene and that individuals were going to have a chance to grow up, to individuate. In the process, the shadow as he called it, would emerge and express itself. In Christian terms he refers to this as the archetype of the Antichrist.

You could say, as we look out over the world scene with the war on terrorism, with 9-11 and so on, with the conflict in the Middle East, and the AIDS pandemic and so forth, that we are seeing the shadow expressing itself. Equally it is expressing in our individual lives, each person on their own, struggling with their own unique expression of the shadow, whether that be through addiction, illness, violence, neurosis, unrest, or whatever.

71

So, instead of seeing Christ coming as an external person, we see Christ come in the individual. This can come as quite a shock if you're not expecting it. The Self as it seeks to make itself known may not come gently. This is the knowing as we have spoken in this talk, and elsewhere in this book, of our being more than just this limited human. Its coming may cause psychic upheaval. It may generate feelings of "fear and trembling" in the hearts and minds of the subject. On top of this, seeing events unfolding on the world scene may have the same effect.

All of these happenings can be called "apocalyptic," in the sense that apocalypse means "uncovering." Something is being revealed here. But the thing to remember is that the coming of the Self is Good News. If I may use a metaphor, its like humanity is going through a big car wash right now and we're on the rinse cycle.

J: That's a good one. As long as we come out spot free.

A: But I want to say that I feel it's important to maintain an attitude of hopefulness and optimism and to keep an eye on the bigger picture. It's easy to be pulled down by fear and negativity but that is not the way of Christ. Love and hopefulness are, and I think it's important to stay on that side of things and not let your self be sucked in by fear. Little by little as the Self comes through, courage replaces fear and one comes to see and to be in the light.

J: If we can remember to always have just a little bit more compassion.

Epilogue

This book can do no more than give the reader a hint at the evolution that took place for me in the year and a half that John and I worked together.

Apart from the conversations there was daily life. John showed me, in his own way, something about what it meant to practice what he was talking about. I began to see God, or the Self, as not only to be sought within, but as that which was reflected in the world around me.

I began to grasp that the events of my life and the expressions of the Mind, some beautiful, some not so pleasant, were expressions of the Self and that the phenomena was indeed there to teach me. The divine that I had spent a decade preaching about in the church began to dwarf in comparison to what I was learning and yet was essentially still included. There is a somewhat obscure Christian term called "panentheism" (as opposed to "pantheism") which expresses that God is to be found in all and in more than that. This was part of what I was learning – not just with my intellect, but with my whole being.

John was showing a solitary way. It isn't easy and, as he has said, there is initially a need for someone to encourage and support you in the process. He was there to do that. I especially needed encouragement to play and there was always something in the works, whether going to see a movie, going out to eat or going to the beach. But these activities bore the stamp of contemplative practice. I was encouraged to look, to see, to think and to reflect.

This is a book to be reflected upon and gone over. And yet it is meant to be no more than a beginning, an introduction.

I thank God, Buddha and the Universe for bringing John and me together to do this work.

About the Co-Authors

Ashley C. Neal

The Rev. Ashley Neal was born in England in 1952 and came to the United States for the first time in 1955 and again in 1961, after a period of living in Europe. Ashley has long felt that the essential teachings of Jesus would have to include the essence of other world religions to be viable. She became interested at an early age in some of those religions and read about Confucianism, Tibetan Buddhism and the <u>Bhagavad</u> <u>Gita</u> seeking to learn more. She would nevertheless pursue her path within the framework of the Christian church.

After an early career in business, Ashley felt drawn to the ordained ministry. She received her Master's of Divinity from Yale Divinity School, where she was particularly interested in theology and biblical studies.

Ashley was ordained an Episcopal priest in 1991. She has served in parish ministry in New Jersey and Florida and also pursued ecumenical and inter-religious dialogue. During those years, she served as Ecumenical Officer for her diocese (Newark, N.J.,) and had the opportunity to dialogue with members of the Bah'ai and Sikh traditions, as well as to work closely with other Christian denominations.

This is Ashley's first book.

John C. Seniff

*I have always felt that there were many
paths and different approaches to God. Nothing
needs to be narrowed down to this or that- yet it
is not so good to mix things up too much either.
Essentially it's about your self and nothing but
your self, and in Minding that inner strength. If
one gets caught up in or leans on different
practices believing that will help him or her to
attain Self-realization or find God, one is, I think,
sadly missing the boat.*

-John C. Seniff

Rev. John (Pure Sound) Seniff was born in Columbus, Ohio in 1954 and lived there and in northern Florida until moving to Asia at the age of 8, (India, Thailand, Philippines) where he spent the next ten years. During those formative years in India, John was greatly influenced by the Hindu myths and stories. He later moved to London where he was introduced to Zen Buddhism through the writings of the Anglican priest, Alan Watts. This was a turning point in his life. Returning to the States in the 1970's, he and philosopher/writer Ken Wilber began one of this country's early meditation groups.

At the age of 19 he met his Zen teacher, Rev. Seikan Hasegawa and began formal study with him. After several months, John decided to leave and explore his Christian roots. He spent time at the Benedictine Grange, an experimental monastic community in Maine founded by Brother David Steindl-Rast. After a period of exploring a vocation, John decided that while there were elements that he could incorporate into his practice, monastic life was not for him.

John would later begin a branch of the Rock Creek Buddhist Temple (affiliated with Rev. Hasegawa) in Tallahassee, Florida. Then, after a career as a graphic artist in Washington DC, he moved to Santa Fe, New Mexico where he received a Masters degree in psychotherapy. He worked in various clinical settings as well as in private practice in New Mexico, while continuing his spiritual training.

On his journey, John has met various teachers from different traditions as well as those not affiliated with a traditional path. He has been strongly influenced by the teachings of Ramana Maharshi, Maharaj Nisargadatta and J. Krishnamurti.

John has stayed in contact with his Zen teacher throughout his life, and in 1997 was ordained a Buddhist priest, in the Mahayana tradition. This is John's first book. His second, a spiritual autobiography, traces his adventures through New Mexico and India.

Notes

i Bohm, David, Nichol, Lee (Ed.), On Dialogue, Routledge, N.Y., 1999, p.12.

ii Hasegawa, Seikan, The Cave of Poison Grass, Great Ocean Publishers, Arlington, Va., 1975, p.7.

iii Hasegawa, Op.Cit., p. 95.

iv The Oxford Annotated Bible,Op.Cit., p. 149, NT.

v Johnston, William (Ed.), The Cloud of Unknowing, Image Books, N.Y., 1996, p.96.

vi The New Oxford Annotated Bible, Op, Cit., p. 66, AP.

vii Sri Nisargadatta Maharaj, I Am That, Kavi Arya. D. Phil (Oxon), for Chatana (P.) Ltd., Bombay, India, 1999, pp. 180-181.

viii Ibid.

ix Radical Awakening, Cutting Through the Conditioned Mind; Dialogues with Stephen Jourdain, Edited by Gilles Farcet, Inner Directions Publishing, Carlsbad, Calif. 2001.

x Oxford Annotated Bible, Op. Cit., p. 72, OT.

xi I Am That, Op.Cit., p. 125.

xii Cave of Poison Grass,Op.Cit., p. 171.

xiii Oxford Annotated Bible, p. 281, NT.